# WEAVING

*by* KARIN KELLY    *pictures by* GEORGE OVERLIE

Lerner Publications Company • Minneapolis, Minnesota

LIBRARY OF CONGRESS CATALOGING IN PUBLICATION DATA

Kelly, Karin.
  Weaving.

  (An Early Craft Book)
  SUMMARY: Simple instructions for making several kinds
of looms and weaving on them, with suggestions for various
projects.

  1. Hand weaving—Juvenile literature. [1. Hand weaving. 2.
Weaving. 3. Handicraft] I. Overlie, George, illus.  II. Title.

TT848.K44                 746.1′4                 72-13336
ISBN 0-8225-0861-3

# Contents

# A long time ago

The craft of weaving began with the dawn of civilization. The hand loom, or frame upon which cloth is woven, was one of man's earliest tools. Four thousand years ago, when Egypt became a fabulous and cultured nation, beautiful cloth was already common.

About two hundred years ago, power looms were invented. Because power looms could make many yards of smooth, perfect cloth very quickly, cloth manufacturing became an important modern industry.

But some people did not want to give up weaving on hand looms. They knew that hand-woven cloth was often prettier than machine-woven cloth. And it was their personal creation.

Many of our great-great-grandmothers wove their own cloth. If they lived in the country, they

tended sheep and clipped their wool to make yarn. They cleaned the wool and spun the yarn on spinning wheels. Then they used the yarn to make woolen cloth that was sturdy and plain, or soft and light as a fluffy kitten.

# How cloth is made

Let's learn how to make a piece of cloth. You will see very soon that you get a special kind of satisfaction from your work. Weaving is rhythmic. As your thread goes in and out and in and out, let your thoughts drift with it. Think about pleasing natural rhythms like the rhythm of the waves rolling onto the beach or the rhythms of your days from sunrise to sunset.

Look at the shirt or dress you are wearing. Is it cotton or woolen cloth? Is it nylon or some other man-made material? If it has been woven, when you look at it closely you will see that it is made of small strings of thread that criss-cross one another. The threads that run up and down are called warp threads. The threads that cross them are called weft or woof threads.

When you weave a piece of cloth, the warp threads are held firmly on a loom. You weave the weft threads in and out through them.

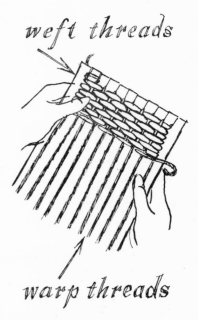

weft threads

warp threads

7

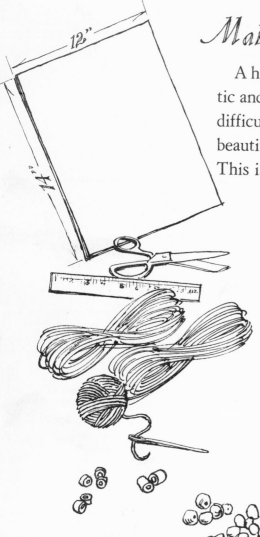

# Making a loom

A hand loom is made of wood, metal, or plastic and has many different parts. It is somewhat difficult to work with. But you can weave a beautiful cloth on a loom made of cardboard. This is what you will need:

a piece of heavy cardboard that is 14 inches long and 12 inches wide (After you have learned how to make a loom, you can work with any size cardboard you like.)

a scissors

a ruler

35 to 40 yards of bulky yarn in several different colors for the weft

a ball of two-ply jute or strong string for the warp

a tapestry needle (A tapestry needle has a big eye and a blunt point.)

wooden, clay, or plastic beads to match the yarn.

Now you can begin to make your loom. Use a ruler and draw a line one-half inch down from the top of the cardboard. Draw another line one-half inch up from the bottom of the cardboard. Then mark off both of those lines at half-inch intervals. You can do this by putting dots at every half inch. When the lines are marked, draw lines from the dots to the edges of the cardboard.

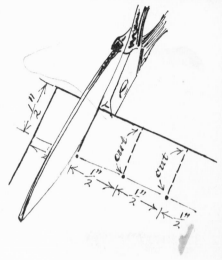

Then cut on the half-inch lines from the edge of the cardboard to the lines you have drawn across the top and bottom. After you have finished cutting, you will have 24 tabs at the top and bottom of the cardboard. Be careful so that you do not bend or tear the cardboard as you cut. The cardboard must remain firm so that you will have a strong background for your weaving.

When you have made the cuts on the top and the bottom of the cardboard, you can string the warp, or up-and-down threads. For the warp, you will use the ball of jute or string. As you learn more about weaving, you will find other kinds of threads that can be used as warp. You

ready for stringing

*push in firmly*

*wind around
second tab*

*pull gently
to bottom*

can use strong crochet thread, cotton rug warp, or even the wool yarn that you use for weft. If you use the yarn, your finished cloth will have a checkered appearance because the warp is the same size as the weft and will show in the fabric.

Hold the cardboard so that the cuts are at the top and bottom. Take one end of the jute, or warp thread, and push it down from the front firmly into the first cut so that the loose end sticks out of the back of the cardboard on the top left. Wind the jute around the second tab three or four times. When the warp thread is again coming out of the front of the cut, tighten it gently and then pull the length of the string all the way down the front of the cardboard to the bottom. Push the warp thread firmly into the first cut at the bottom of the cardboard. Wind it once around the back of the second tab until it shows at the front of the second cut. Tighten the warp gently and pull the warp thread to the top again. Wind it once around the back of the third tab at the top.

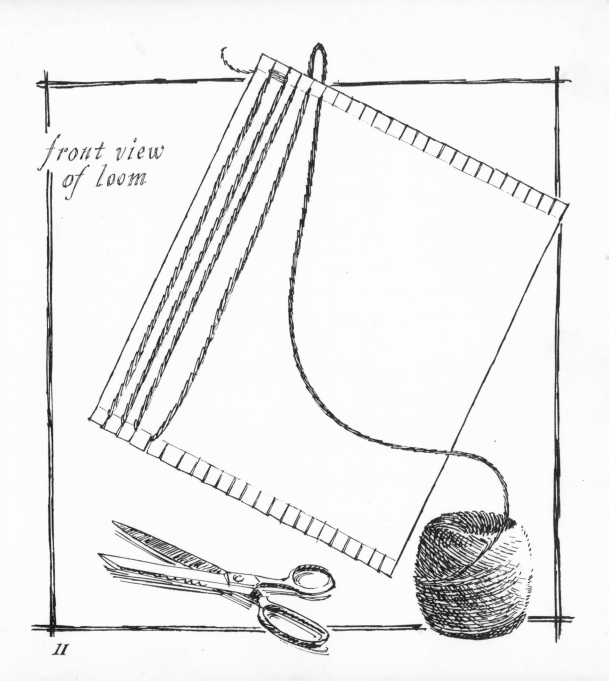

*front view
of loom*

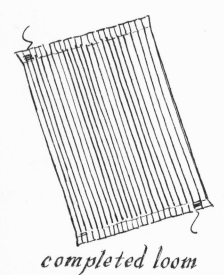

*completed loom*

*weft a different color*

You should wind the warp string around every other tab at the top and bottom of the cardboard until you come to the second-to-the-last tab at the bottom right. As you wind, be sure that the warp strings are tight and smooth. Wind the warp string around the second-to-the-last tab at the bottom three or four times. Cut the warp loose from the ball. Now you will have 23 warp strings wound firmly around the tabs on your cardboard loom. You are ready to begin weaving the weft.

Weaving the weft is the most satisfying part of weaving cloth. When you have woven only eight or ten strands of weft, you will begin to see the pattern of the fabric.

The first piece of cloth you make on the cardboard loom will have fringes on both sides. Because you are using heavy yarn, it would be difficult to make cloth that is bound on all edges. If you were weaving with lighter-weight yarn, you could use a shuttle, or spool, to carry long lengths of weft with you as you wove.

What colors have you chosen? Do you like colors that look like colors from nature? Have you chosen brown, or gold, or autumn red? Or do you like bright, eye-catching colors? Do you have bright pink, or orange, or purple? You can make several cloths that are very different from one another by using only three colors. You can make stripes, or you can make multicolored fabric by using different pieces of yarn each time you weave. A design for your cloth will probably take shape in your mind as you begin to weave.

Choose the color you would like to use for the first stripe in your cloth. If the yarn is in a skein, that is, if it looks like it is wound in large loops, you should unwind the skein and rewind the yarn into a nice round ball. If you do not, the yarn might become tangled and you will become impatient when you want to cut it into short lengths.

*skein of yarn*

Have a friend put his hands in the skein at each end of the loop. Look in the center of the skein for the place where the ends of the yarn

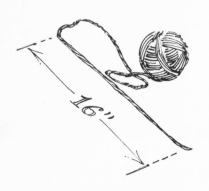

*wind into a ball*

have been tied together. Cut the ends apart and begin to wind one of the loose ends around your fingers. When you have wound the yarn around your fingers 20 times, slip the yarn off and wind in the opposite direction. You can also use the back of a straight chair to hold the skein while you are winding.

When you have chosen your first color, you may begin to cut the weft strips. Your loom is 12 inches wide, so you will need yarn longer than 12 inches in order to make a nice fluffy fringe. Cut the yarn into 16-inch pieces so that you will have a two-inch fringe on each side. You do not need to measure each piece with a ruler. Measure the first piece, cut it, and then hold it up and measure and cut the rest of the pieces so that they are the same length as the first.

To make a stripe in your cloth that is about two-and-a-half inches wide, you will need about 20 strips of yarn. You will save time if you cut all 20 strips before you begin. Then, after you begin weaving, you can cut and weave as you wish to vary your task.

# Learning to weave

To weave in the weft with bulky yarn, the only tool you will need is your fingers. Begin at the top of the loom. Take one end of the first strip and weave it *over* the first string in the warp. Weave it under the second string and over the third string and under the fourth string and so on until you come to the end of the row of warp strings. Pull the yarn so that there is an even amount of fringe at both sides of the loom. Then push the yarn very tightly against the top of the warp threads. This is called "beating" the weft.

Take another strip of yarn. This time, weave it *under* the first warp string and over the second and under the third and so on until you come to the end. Push it tightly against the first weft thread. When you weave your third strip of yarn, weave it over the first warp string and under the second as you did with the first yarn strip. You should weave over the first warp string with every other weft yarn. Push each one tightly against the weft before it. If you make a

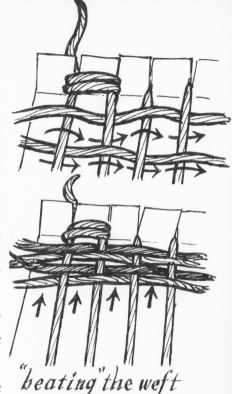

"beating" the weft

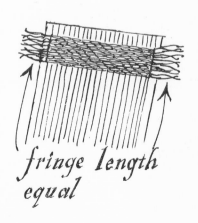

fringe length equal

mistake and weave two weft threads the same way, take the second one out right away. If you do not, it will show on your finished cloth.

After you have woven in eight or ten yarn strips, you can begin to see what the cloth you are weaving will look like. The warp threads will begin to blend with the weft and the cloth will look like the cloth you are used to seeing.

The piece of cloth you weave with bulky yarn would look very nice as a wall hanging. Because it will hang on a wall and not get hard use like the cloth in your dress or shirt, you can add decorations to the cloth. You can weave in beads, feathers, dried flowers or grasses, pine cones, acorns, or peanut shells that you have pierced with a heavy needle or nail. Look in the tool box for nuts or washers that might suit your fabric. Do you have any broken toys with interesting parts that can be strung on a length of yarn? You can weave in the decorations wherever you think they will look best. Perhaps some will look nice in your second stripe.

*first string beads on weft*

To weave in beads or nuts, you must first string them on a piece of weft yarn. Now you will need the tapestry needle. Thread the needle with the weft thread and then string the beads on it with the needle. Do you have medium-sized beads? String five or more of them on the weft yarn. Then weave the weft into the warp as you have done before. With the beads on the weft, it will not pass smoothly over and under the strings of the warp. Therefore, you must pick up every other warp string to allow the beads to pass under it. After you have woven the weft yarn through the warp, arrange the beads evenly across it. With five beads, for example, you would have a bead at about every fourth warp string. Push the weft yarn with the beads on it tightly against the weft before it. Then weave in more strips of weft. You will soon see that the beads blend into the cloth perfectly.

After you have filled about three-fourths of the warp with weft yarn, you should turn your loom around and begin to weave at the opposite end. If you do not, you will find that the warp at the bottom becomes very tight as the weft is woven closer to it. If you work from the bottom up toward the cloth you have already woven, the warp threads in the middle will stay loose so that you can pick them up with your fingers.

When you have woven in all of the weft that your loom will hold, you can blend all of the threads together. If there is warp showing where you stopped weaving, push all of the weft threads in the loom down and up to make your weaving look even. But you should pack the warp so tightly with weft that when you finish blending the weft yarn, there will be no traces of empty warp.

Now you can remove your finished cloth from the loom. You must be very careful when you do this so that you do not cut the warp threads. If you do, your cloth will fall apart.

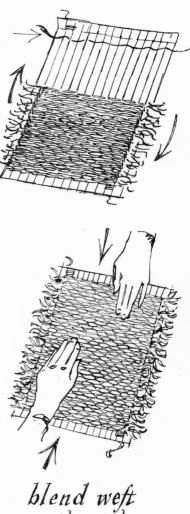

*blend weft threads*

*carefully trim tabs*

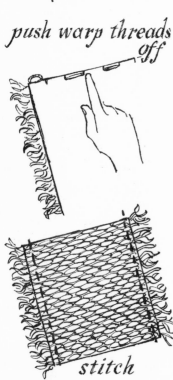

*push warp threads off*

*stitch*

To remove the finished cloth, you must destroy your loom. This is not very serious because it is easy and cheap to make another one. Turn the loom around to the back. You will see where the warp threads are hooked on to the cardboard tabs. Take a scissors and cut the tabs away very carefully. *Do not cut the warp threads.* When you have cut away all of the tabs, gently push the warp threads off the stubs from the tabs. There will be an extra length of warp string at the top right and the bottom left of the cloth. Thread this extra warp in the tapestry needle and weave it in and out through the back of the finished fabric. This will hold the end securely, and it will look nicer than if you simply tied it.

Now you can turn your cloth around and admire it. You have probably admired it a hundred times already, but now you can be really proud. Your fabric is finished! If you would like to make your piece of cloth last a very long time, have a friend stitch the fringed sides with a sewing machine.

**20**

Would you like to hang your fabric? There are many ways to fix it so that it will stay straight when it is hanging. Here is a very simple way. Cut a half-inch strip of cardboard from what is left of your loom. Fold the top of the cloth over the strip just enough so that the cardboard doesn't show. Then sew the cardboard into the fabric. Put in a tiny stitch at the top of the cloth and over the cardboard, and the cloth will stay flat for hanging.

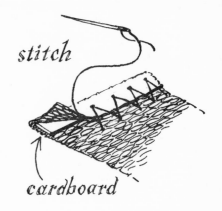

*stitch*

*cardboard*

You can also use a pretty piece of driftwood, an interesting stick, or bamboo to hang your fabric. Tack the cloth onto the wood with very small nails or sew it on with warp string.

Weft yarn makes a fine hanger. Cut a piece of weft about 14 inches long. Thread it on the tapestry needle. Push the needle through the cloth from back to front near the fringe on one side. String a bead on the yarn, slip the needle off the yarn, and put a knot in the end of it. Pull the bead and knot firmly against the front of the fabric. Thread the needle again with the

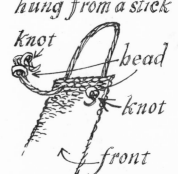

*hung from a stick*

*knot*

*bead*

*knot*

*front*

loose end of the yarn hanger. Push the needle through the cloth from back to front at the other end of the cloth. String a bead on the yarn, slip the needle off, and knot the yarn. Tighten the bead and knot as you did the first time. Now you may hang your fabric wherever you like.

## *Weaving with a shuttle*

As you learn to make better and prettier wall hangings, you might want to learn how to use more complicated tools. Through the centuries, weavers have had many brilliant ideas about how to make their cloth more perfect and how to make it useful for many different things. One of the earliest weaving inventions, besides the loom, was the shuttle. The shuttle is a kind of spool that helps the weaver to carry long lengths of weft with him as he weaves it into the warp.

If you learn to make and use a shuttle, you can make cloth that is bound on all sides and not fringed as your wall hangings are. You would soon see how important a shuttle was if you

*weft on spool*

*shuttle*

tried to weave a piece of fabric that was finished on all sides using only your fingers or a needle. You could not carry much weft with your fingers or a needle, and you would run out of it every three or four lines. You would have to cut new lengths of weft very often, and with fine yarn, it would take a long time to finish a piece of cloth.

Let's make a long strip of bound cloth with fine yarn and a shuttle. You can use the strip for many things. You can use it for a belt, a headband, or a bookmark. You can sew bells on the bottom of it and hang it on your door at holiday time.

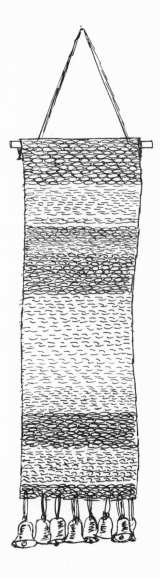

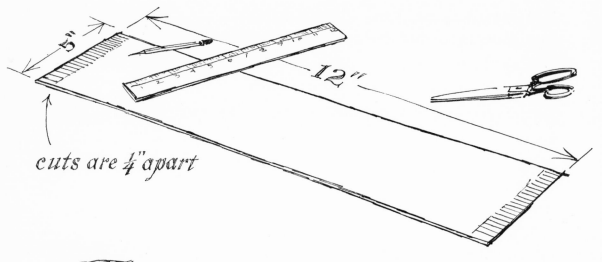

cuts are ⅟₄" apart

sweater yarn

bulky yarn

To make the cloth strip, you will again use a cardboard loom. You can use the two-ply jute or cotton rug warp for warp, but you will need a finer yarn for the weft. A yarn that is used to make a regular sweater would be a good-sized yarn for the cloth strip. Sweater yarn is called three-ply or four-ply yarn. When you go to the store to choose the colors you like, you can see both sizes and can choose the one you like the best.

To make your new cardboard loom, cut out a

piece of cardboard that is about twelve inches long and five inches wide. This size loom will make a nice bell strip. You can make a narrower loom for a headband or bookmark. Measure the cardboard and cut notches as you did for the wall hanging, but this time make the cuts about one-quarter inch apart. Start the first notch one-half inch from the edge of the cardboard. After you have strung the warp, you will see that your finished cloth strip will be four inches wide.

When the warp has been strung, tape the tabs together at the top and bottom of the loom with cellophane or masking tape so that they do not tear or become loose as you weave.

Because you will be using a bulky shuttle, you should separate the warp from the cardboard. This will make it easier for you to weave the shuttle over and under the warp strings. From a piece of lightweight cardboard, cut a rectangle six inches long and one inch wide. Fold the rectangle the long way into a V shape. Insert it between the warp threads and the cardboard, and move it down as you weave.

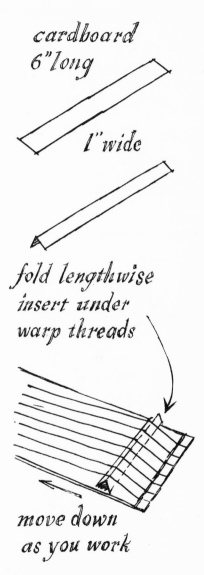

*cardboard 6" long*

*1" wide*

*fold lengthwise insert under warp threads*

*move down as you work*

**25**

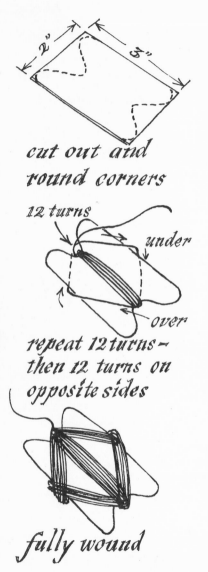

*cut out and round corners*

12 turns

under

over

*repeat 12 turns – then 12 turns on opposite sides*

*fully wound*

When the warp is strung, you can begin to prepare the weft. Now you must make a shuttle. You can cut the shuttle out of cardboard too. First cut a small rectangle out of cardboard that is two inches wide and three inches long. Cut the corners so that they are round and smooth. Then cut curved notches in the ends of the rectangle.

Now you can wind about three yards of the weft yarn onto the shuttle. First wind the yarn around the flat surfaces between the "legs" of the shuttle. Then wind it from the ends to the edges. You might want to make and wind several shuttles with different colors of yarn. When your shuttles are wound, you may begin to weave.

Before you weave the first line of weft, unwind about six inches of yarn from the shuttle. Then weave the shuttle *over* the first warp thread and under the second and over the third and so on until you come to the edge of the warp. Leave a few inches of weft loose at the edge of the loom where you began. You can

26

weave this fringe into your fabric when you have finished.

As you weave, the weft yarn will follow along after the shuttle. When you come to the edge of the warp, pull the weft down diagonally. Push it gently but tightly against the top of the warp with your fingers. Unroll a few more inches of yarn from the shuttle. Then, starting from the edge of the warp where your shuttle is, weave *under* the first warp string and over the second and under the third and so on until you get back to the edge where you began weaving. Pull the weft diagonally again and push it against the weft before it. After you have woven several rows, you can use a wide-toothed comb or a fork to push the weft into place.

Continue weaving until almost all of the thread on the shuttle has been used. After you have woven the last complete line that you can with your length of yarn, let the end of the yarn hang loose at the edge of the warp. Begin weaving a new line, but again leave a few inches of

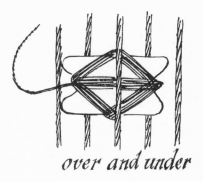

*over and under*

*push weft up gently*

*use wide toothed comb*

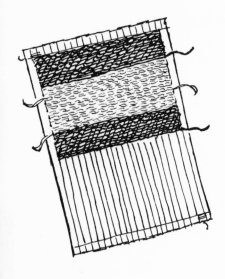

yarn loose at the edge of the fabric. You can weave all of these loose ends into the warp with a tapestry needle when you have finished your cloth.

When you have come to the end of the warp threads, you can also weave in the loose ends of the warp as you did with your wall hanging. Did you make a striped cloth this time? Did you use many colors?

You can make a wall hanging that looks like a face. Make a cardboard loom and begin the top of the face by weaving in strips of bulky yarn. Cut long strips of yarn so that you have four-inch fringes on each side. The fringes will hang down and look like hair. When you begin to weave the face itself, weave with finer yarn and a shuttle so that the rest of the piece has a bound edge.

When you come to the spot in the cloth where the mouth will be, weave in some bulky yarn again, but weave it through only six or eight of the middle warp threads. Let the fringes hang from the middle of the piece of cloth. They

will look like a droopy moustache. Blend weft threads of the finer yarn around the bulky yarn moustache. You can weave in chin whiskers at the bottom. After the cloth is finished, sew on buttons or beads to look like eyes, nose, and mouth.

## A wooden loom

When you have learned to make the simple kinds of fabrics that have been described in this book, you will be well on your way toward learning how to work with a more complicated wooden loom. You can make a simple one yourself. Get four pieces of one-by-two-inch pine board. Get two pieces that are 14 inches long and two pieces that are 18 inches long. Ask a friend to drill one-quarter-inch holes in the ends of the boards. Bolt the boards together tightly with one-and-three-quarter-inch bolts and "wing" nuts. Bolt the 14-inch boards on top of the 18-inch boards. Put the nuts on so that they can be tightened from the top of the loom. Wing nuts are easy to tighten when necessary.

Then mark the 14-inch boards at one-half-inch intervals with a pencil. Drive one-and-one-half-inch finishing nails into the boards at the points you have marked. Drive them in straight and deep so that an inch of nail sticks up. You will string the warp around these nails.

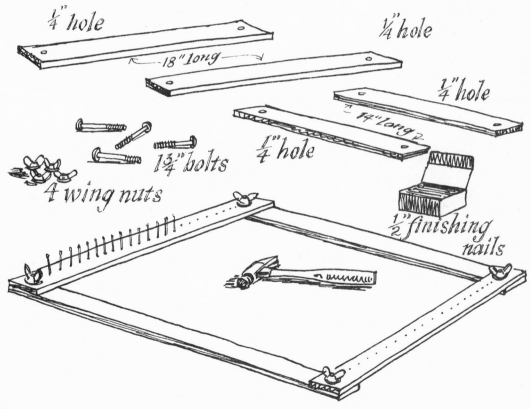

$\frac{1}{4}$" hole

$\frac{1}{4}$" hole

← 18" long →

$\frac{1}{4}$" hole

14" long

$\frac{1}{4}$" hole

$1\frac{3}{4}$" bolts

4 wing nuts

$1\frac{1}{2}$" finishing nails

# Other projects

Whether you use cardboard looms or a simple wooden loom, you can make fabrics that you can use for many things. You can make a pillow out of a fringed fabric. Sew another piece of cloth onto the back of the cloth and stuff the area inside with dacron fluff or with nylon stockings that have been cut into one-inch rings. You can make place mats for the table or potholders for the kitchen from cotton rug yarn. You can attach several pieces of fabric together and make a simple vest or poncho. You can make a sack out of a piece of fabric and put a strap on it so that you can use it as a school bag. Cloth can be used in so many ways. Just use your imagination.

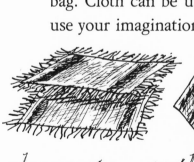

*hand bag + place mats + potholders + pillows*